I0845819

Chiseled Devotion

Exploring Carved Out Temples

Table of Contents

Chapter 1. Introduction

Immerse yourself in a remarkable journey through time, art, and devout perseverance as we explore the marvel of human dedication in our Special Report, "Chiseled Devotion: Exploring Carved Out Temples". This astonishing journey takes you deep into the living heart of stone, into the delicate artistry which created some of the most breathtaking architecture in the world. Our report will unveil the stories hidden within ancient hallowed walls, providing an awe-inspiring view of mankind's enduring devotion, carved out in stone. Unravel how these timeless edifices were shaped, the legends behind their construction, and how they still resonate with an energetic spiritual vibration to this day. Get ready to embrace history, culture, and human achievement as never before. Don't miss out on this exciting adventure; it will not only entertain but also fill you with a renewed appreciation for the depth of our shared human heritage! Buy this Special Report now, and join us as we dive into artistic epochs where spiritual belief met chisel and stone, creating miracles in architecture.

Chapter 2. The World Beneath the Chisel: An Introduction

Your journey starts here, in the realm of devotion and art so pure and potent, it rivals the vocabulary of expression. In an age where grand constructions were an outward reflection of one's commitment to a higher power and to unattainable ideals, ancient civilizations were given a tangible existence through sculptures carved with such devotion that they stands as an eternal testament to their makers' unwavering faith.

2.1. The Journey of a Single Stone

Every endeavor begins with a single step and, in this context, it commences with a single stone. Roughly hewn from the living earth, this primeval resource was transformed by craft and human determination into eternal legacies of beauty and devotion.

This is not just about the labor or technical skill involved. It's an exploration of the deep spiritual implications and the sanctity of intent behind each stroke of the chisel. Every chip made by the mason contributed to the greater purpose, representing a symphony of human will and quintessential faith, played out upon the canvas of raw stone. It would ultimately give birth to structures that continue to inspire, filling onlookers with awe and reverence, years and even millennia after their creation.

2.2. The Silent Narratives

As you wander through these labyrinthine constructs of mortal endeavor, note the stories these silent edifices narrate; Stories of valor, sacrifice, love, and spiritual evolution. The intricate details etched into walls are silent, yet they sing songs of ancient yore. The carved reliefs bring to life tales of legendary figures, gods and demigods, the origin of the universe, and time itself.

Unveiling these narratives brings forth profound insights into the historical and cultural context in which these structures were crafted. It unveils the mindset of a civilization, their beliefs, and their everyday lives. The very stone that makes up these grand temples houses a treasure trove of chronicles waiting to be deciphered by those curious enough to listen.

2.3. Legends of Their Time

Review these marvels not as mere lifeless structures, but the result of human emotion compressed into material form. The chipped stone and weathered pathways manifest the stories of countless individuals. The masons drawn from the vast spectrum of societal hierarchies, from the royals who commissioned these majestic temples to the robust laborers who broke their backs turning ambition into reality.

Walk in their shoes and glean a deeper insight into the tales of these unseen hands. Their stories are intricately woven into the fabric of these magnificent structures as seamlessly as the stories of gods and goddesses they adored and revered.

2.4. Bridges to the Divine

These architectural wonders continue to serve as conduits to the divine, resonating with vibrations that transcend the limits of time and space. The grand sanctum at the heart of each temple, often housing the deity, emits an intangible energy recognized and felt by all who have the privilege of experiencing it.

The meticulous design principles underlying these structures often encapsulate the singular purpose of uniting the material and the spiritual. The artistic harmony seen in the arrangement of carved space and solid stone is believed to serve a cosmic function - amplifying the spiritual energy within the sanctum and radiating it to the surrounding environment.

This exploration is not merely an academic exercise. Rather, it is a leap of faith. A dive into the ocean of human perseverance and a reflection of the universal quest for the divine. If one listens closely, the silent stones echo the persistent pulse of human longing for the infinite.

By seeking to comprehend the meaning behind these noble endeavors, we hope to bring forth a profound appreciation for our shared human heritage and the boundless potentials of the human spirit when fueled by unshakable faith and devotion. We offer you this doorway, this threshold to walk upon the grounds of ancient lore and to feel the pulsating energetic ripples of how belief met chisel and stone, shaping untold miraculous epochs in architectural history.

As you progress through this journey, each step further will gradually reveal the grandeur of these edifices, throwing light on how humanity brazenly etched its indomitable spirit into the heart of stone, creating architectural symphonies that continue singing odes to the devoted hearts that gave them form.

Chapter 3. Awakening Stone: Early Carved Temples

Our journey begins at the dawn of civilization, where early societies set forth to express their religious and spiritual beliefs in artistic and architectural form. In order to comprehend how the ancient art of temple-making came to be, one must understand the sociopolitical climate of that era and the progression of early spiritual beliefs across various societies. The delicate craftsmanship seen in these temples is a testament to the enduring perseverance of humankind and their devotion to their spiritual beliefs.

3.1. The Birth of Spiritual Architecture

There lies an intrinsic connection between humanity's spiritual beliefs and built environments, which emerged as soon as our ancestors transitioned from nomadic lifestyles to more sedentary practices. These early settlers discovered the advantages of construction and began to define individual spaces for varied uses. Spiritual beliefs played a significant role in shaping these spaces. This advanced further when societies began to see the necessity for elaborate, specifically designated spaces to pay homage to their gods and engage in religious observances.

It was during the Bronze Age, approximately 3000 BC, when the first temples were constructed, and they began as modest, earthbound structures. These rudimentary spiritual centers were made from readily available materials like earth, wood, or thatch. Their simplicity, however, should not undermine the remarkable leap they represented in human architectural ingenuity.

3.2. Evolution to Stone Temples

As societies became more complex and their technological capabilities advanced, so too did their architecture. There was a shift from wood and thatch to the considerably more resilient medium of stone, primarily due to two reasons. Stone was not only more durable, but also symbolized the impenetrable and immortal nature of the gods these societies worshipped.

Emerging in the late Bronze Age and continuing into the Iron Age, around 1300 BC, the usage of megaliths – large, prehistoric stones used for constructing monuments or buildings – became widespread.

The Greeks and Egyptians, among other ancient societies, were noted for their early adoption of stone in their religious architecture. Historical data suggests that the shift to stone structures was both practical and symbolic, embodying a society's evolution in craftsmanship and its advanced comprehension of mortality, permanence, and the divine.

3.3. Greek Parthenon: A Testament to Perseverance and Skill

The Greek Parthenon, an amazing structure well-revered for its size and grandeur, stands as a testament to early temple architecture. The construction of this magnificent edifice reflects the deep spiritual devotion and architectural prowess of the Greeks. Cut exclusively from marble, every part of the Parthenon, right down to its most minute detail, exhibits unparalleled craftsmanship.

The temple was built to house a colossal statue of Athena Parthenos, the patron goddess Athena depicted in her most virgin form. The temple's facade, however, held more than just the enormous statue. The metopes, carved panels adorning the upper part of the Parthenon, depict mythical battles that symbolized the societal values and religious beliefs of the Greeks. These artistically rich carvings are testaments of the narrative power of stone, imbibed with the Greeks' spiritual fervor and dedication.

3.4. Egyptian Temples: The Cosmological Connection

Moving towards the African continent, ancient Egyptian temples played a similar role as a nucleus of religious activities, albeit with their own unique architectural designs and significance. These structures, usually aligned with the cosmos, carry a profound cosmological connection, reflecting the Egyptians' belief in the cosmic order, or Ma'at.

Egyptian temples, like the Luxor and Karnak temples, were often grand in size and meticulously sculpted, reminding us of the great heights human dedication and perseverance can reach when fueled by deep spiritual beliefs. These edifices were created not just as a dwelling for the deities, but also as an embodiment of the cosmic order, a harmonious balance between chaos and stability. In accordance with this belief, every aspect of these temples was intentional, designed with the aim to imbue in their worshippers a sense of divine awe and reverence.

3.5. Conclusion

The early carved stone temples marked a turning point in human civilization. Their transcendent beauty embodied not just the height of architectural prowess of the time, but also stood as a symbol of spiritual reverence and human aspiration.

The meticulous carvings in these temples, rich with symbols and narratives, have shared with us stories across millennia, revealing the depth and sophistication of early human consciousness, its perennial quest for meaning, and the unyielding yearning to transcend the transitory nature of life.

Through these edifices carved out of stone, human devotion found a medium to immortalize its faith and beliefs. And thus, these timeless structures continue to resonate with a profound spiritual vibration, providing a testament to human achievement, dedication, and the undying pursuit of divinity.

Chapter 4. Spirit in Stone: Symbolism and Iconography

Entering an ancient temple instills a sense of being part of something larger than oneself, a timeless connection that seamlessly binds the human experience regardless of era or location. The sensation is created in no small part by the temples' architecture but a significant contributor to this transcendence is the complex language of symbols and iconography etched into stone.

4.1. The Language of Stone

Symbols and iconography are universal methods of communication, often representing complex concepts, ideas, and beliefs, transcending the barriers of languages. They serve as coded messages, visually translating the spiritual tenets of religion into tangible forms. The art on temple walls is much more than static decorations; it forms a compelling narrative that unfolds before the eyes of the beholder, rich with information about the era, the religion, cultural practices, even sometimes the life of the common man.

4.2. The Significance of Symbolism

Symbolism layered within each temple varies greatly, contingent upon the local culture, time period, and the religion that inspired the structure. It is not uncommon to find symbols representing duality, like light and darkness, masculinity and femininity, death and rebirth, often which represent a cosmic balance. There are also frequent representations of divine entities, plentiful in number and detailed in design, each embodying specific traits or responsibilities within the spiritual doctrine.

Many symbols connect humanity with the divine, acting as bridges between the terrestrial and celestial world. They celebrate the elements of nature—earth, water, fire, air, and space—highlighting our deep-rooted connections with the natural world. With countless variations and intricate relationships, these symbols form an encrypted language, waiting to be deciphered by curious eyes.

4.3. Iconography: A Doorway to the Divine

Alongside symbols, iconography plays a pivotal role in explaining the fundamental tenets of a religion. Statues of revered idols, etched carefully and vividly, not only inspire awe but also provide a tactile reference for worshipers. These representations aren't meant to provide a literal visage of the deity but are skillfully composed aggregations of attributes, characteristics, and symbols that relate to the deified entity.

Each divine figure's iconography encapsulates their unique aspects — their poses, their facial expressions, the number of limbs, the objects they hold, their mount or 'vehicle', and even their adornments. These attributes contribute information about the depicted deity's characteristics, powers, and the fables associated with them, creating an enduring connection between devotees and their divine patrons.

4.4. Decoding the Temples: Case Studies

Exploring specific instances of symbolism and iconography in temples from different parts of the world offers a glimpse into the vast repertoire of these art forms:

4.5. Angkor Wat, Cambodia: The Dance of Gods and Demons

At the heart of the symbolic narrative in Angkor Wat, often considered the epitome of Khmer architecture, one finds the "Churning of the Ocean of Milk". The epic scene, recreated on a massive wall, depicts the gods (devas) and demons (asuras) churning the cosmic ocean, a puranic story from Hinduism. This was to extract the nectar of immortality, beautiful damsels, magnificent beings, and other celestial gifts. The image is not simply a dramatic spectacle of the divine; it represents an intricate cosmological concept, a philosophical conundrum about the constant struggle between good and evil.

4.6. Chartres Cathedral, France: The Gospel in Stone

Chartres Cathedral in France represents Christian iconography at its zenith. The famed Gothic architecture houses more than just worship space. Its statuesque figures, sculpted portals, and stained glass provide a visually compelling narrative of the biblical story. From Adam and Eve in the Garden of Eden to the Crucifixion of Jesus Christ, each figure, scene, and symbol carved on the cathedral's walls serve as elements of a spiritual lesson, visually communicating Christian stories and ideals.

4.7. Pyramid of the Sun, Mexico: Celestial Alignments

In the Mesoamerican pyramids, symbolism converges with astronomy. The Pyramid of the Sun, located at Teotihuacan near Mexico City, integrates spatial and temporal symbolism. The pyramid's alignment with the constellations, specifically the Pleiades, is believed to mark significant agricultural and ceremonial periods. The pyramid's architecture, combined with its celestial alignment, reinforces the ancient civilization's reverence for harmony between celestial and terrestrial realms.

4.8. The Realization

The journey through symbolic narratives in ancient temples underscores the universality of human spiritual enquiry and expression. For millennia, humans have sought to understand, explain, and connect with the divine. Temples, imbued with symbolism and iconography, continue to convey these profound spiritual truths, carrying their impact across centuries. Whether it's the dancing deities of Angkor Wat, the biblical narratives of Chartres Cathedral, or the cosmic connections of Teotihuacan, each one represents a unique geographical and cultural response to the spiritual and metaphysical conundrums of our experience. As understandings of the universe have grown and cosmologies have evolved, so too have these divine structures, constantly re-narrating the age-old story of spiritual pursuit and realisation.

Chapter 5. Architectural Wonders: Techniques and Innovations

The story of humanity's architectural journey is a tale of relentless innovation, ever-changing techniques, and ceaseless adaptation to the prevailing social, cultural, and technological contexts. No journey into the hallowed annals of carved out temples would be complete without exploring this fascinating dimension of human achievement.

5.1. Sculpting the Divine: Early Techniques

In the dawn of time, when the first temples began to be carved out of stone, the techniques applied were as raw and primitive as the crude stones themselves. Using rudimentary tools made from hardened steel, including hammers and chisels, artisans slowly etched their spiritual inspiration into the heart of stone.

The embellishments of these early temples were simple and unsophisticated, a reflection of their tools' limitations and their modest understanding of architectural principles. Still, the determination and the reverence with which these early craftsmen undertook their tasks led to creations that even today inspire awe in their raw power and simplistic beauty.

5.2. Evolving Tools and Techniques

As civilizations evolved and technological knowledge expanded, the instruments used to sculpt spiritual magnificent out of stone evolved too. Bronze tools gave way to iron, and then to steel. Rudimentary hammers and chisels evolved into precision instruments that allowed for more control and greater detail in the sculptures.

Artisans soon developed techniques for polishing the stone, bringing out its natural beauty and providing a greater depth to their creations. They also developed techniques for adding color to the stone, allowing them to bring their works to life in vibrant depictions of the divine.

5.3. Mastery of Structural Dynamics

Structural dynamics began to grow in importance as temples began to increase in size and complexity. The early craftsmen relied on trial and error, littering the landscape with fascinating ruins of grand ambitions. Each failure, however, was a lesson learned. Ancient engineers began to understand the principles of stress and strain and how to distribute the weight of stone to ensure stability.

Temples started to evolve from simple single-room structures to vast edifices that sprawled across several floors and rooms. The development of arches and columns infused these structures with a beauty that amplified the spiritual resonance of the temples.

5.4. Innovation Brought by Different Civilizations

With humanity scattered across different geographic regions, every civilization brought its unique perspective to the art of temple construction. The Egyptians employed simplistic designs, focusing on grandiose sizes, while the Greeks favored intricate sculptures and ornate pediments.

India's temple architecture also saw a progressive evolution from the rock-cut architecture of the Ajanta and Ellora caves to the magnificently intricate stone temples of the South, such as the

Brihadeshwara Temple and the Meenakshi Temple. These innovations were the result of deeply understanding stone's properties, which they adroitly utilized to amplify their devotion.

5.5. The Intricacies of Temple Carving

The craft of temple carving is a meticulous one, demanding patience, skill, and a deep understanding of both the material being used and the divine figures being depicted. The level of detail seen in many temple carvings is truly breathtaking, with even the most minute features brought to vivid life in stone.

Architects and sculptors first sketch rough layouts of their designs, marking the stone with chalk or charcoal. Workers then painstakingly chisel away excess stone bit by bit, revealing the divine forms beneath. As forms become visible, artisans make further refinements, adding details like facial expressions, jewelry, and clothing folds that make these works universes unto themselves.

5.6. The Temple: A Living Legacy

The innovative techniques and methodologies, the evolution of tools and materials, and the adaptation to the various socio-cultural contexts have resulted in the resilient, timeless structures we see today. These temples stand today as a vibrant testament to their makers' indomitable spirit, astute understanding of their environment, and unfathomable devotion to their spiritual beliefs.

This journey has been about more than just appreciating their awe-inspiring beauty. It's a deep dive into the human spirit that could conceptualize, design, and create such magnificent structures out of mere stone. These temples are magnificent texts in stone that immortalize our ancestors' creativity, perseverance, and profound devotion. Therefore, the exploration of these architectural wonders is, invariably, an exploration into the depths of our shared human heritage.

Chapter 6. Empires in Eternity: The Cultural Significance

To perceive the cultural significance of these carved temples does not merely ask for a visceral experience. Instead, it invites a multidimensional understanding combining an awe-inspiring view of ancient architecture, an appreciation of historical civilizations, and an introspection of the spiritual ethos reflected in these structures across diverse geographies.

6.1. Gods and Men: Communion in Stone

The primary intent underscoring the construction of temples was the provision of a sacred space where gods and humans could interact. These were places where the finite met the infinite, where the temporal and the eternal intersected.

Carving temples out of solid rock faces magnified this connection. The choice of location was not random but dictated by what was held as spiritually significant. Sacred mountains, peaceful woods, and the banks of holy rivers often became the chosen ground. Serenity punctuated the air around these sites, providing the devotees a profound experience, far removed from the tumultuousness of life's ordinary course.

6.2. Impression in the Bedrock: Empire Ideologies

Though seemingly religious, these temples often resonate with sociopolitical reverberations. The craftsmanship, intricacies of the design, and scale were not merely a testament to the architects' brilliance but also a reflection of the empire's wealth, power, and ambition. The marked contrast in styles, themes, and deities among temples built during the same era in different regions mirrors the cultural diversity and political ideologies of the distinct empires.

Explicit instances recur in Egyptian, Indian, Mayan, or Greek temples. Pharaohs re-imagined their divine existence in Pyramids, while in India, rock-cut temples like Ellora and Ajanta corresponded to the transition from Vedic ritualistic worship to the Bhakti movement's devotional practice. Similarly, Greek and Mayan temples bore their own distinctive cultural imprints, reflecting the respective empires' ideologies and worldview.

6.3. Land of Paradoxes: Portrayal of Socio-Cultural Narrative

Intricately carved murals and sculptures decorating the temple walls, pillars, and ceilings narrated numerous stories to the worshipers. In the absence of written scripts, these became the mnemonic devices preserving and passing on the socio-cultural narrative. The grandeur and splendor portrayed in these carvings served multiple purposes: they informed, educated, entertained, and most importantly, underlined a worldview that tied the vast empire with a common thread of culture and tradition.

Stories from mythology, scenes of common life, depiction of flora and fauna, astronomical knowledge, to aspects of music, dance and drama encased within these walls shed incredible light on the cultural richness of the respective ancient civilizations.

6.4. A Silent Sermon: The Spiritual Ethos

The temples represented a spiritual ethos that dictated the empire's collective conscience. Symbols and motifs carved out extensively conveyed profound spiritual tenets. The Egyptians emphasized life after death; the Greek moral drama contemplated the boundary between mortals and the divine; Indian temples mirrored the philosophy of Dharma or cosmic order, and Mayan temples celebrated natural cycles and deities' appeasements. This spiritual ethos often acted as the ideological compass, guiding the society's moral and ethical behavior.

6.5. Legacy in Stone: Continuity and Influence

Besides cultural significance, these temples illustrate an enduring legacy. Many of these edifices, despite wars, natural catastrophes, invasions, and the passage of time, continue to command reverence, housing active places of worship. Their influence echoes not just in architectural forms but also in literature, art, music, dance, governance, and jurisprudence across generations and geographies.

The cultural significance of these carved temples transcends space and time, unfolding a universe where the stone speaks, and history lives on. Whether one seeks the divine or merely revels in the artistic majesty, the impact is inescapable as these temples offer an immersive experience of cultural osmosis, transporting one from the realm of the known into a world divine and mystical, forever captured in the eternity of stone.

Chapter 7. The Hands That Shape Divinity: Stories of the Artisans

From the heart of centuries-old forests reverberates the ceaseless sound of chisels striking stone. Driven by a divine passion and an obstinate perseverance, men and women have poured eons of labor into chiseling blocks of ordinary rock into extraordinary temples of worship. These craftsmen, their names lost to history, have blended skill, faith, emotion, and creativity into work of such magnitude that they stand as timeless testaments to collective spiritual yearning and human ability. Their hands, weathered by time and toil, have achieved the seemingly impossible task of coaxing divinity from stone.

7.1. The Light in the Stone

In their hands, stone was not just an inert material; it was a canvas that held within it the potential to reveal the divine. The transformative journey from a bland block into a detailed sculpture was seen not as a mere artistic process but as a transformative, divine undertaking. The craftsmen did not impose themselves, but gently coaxed the light from within the stone, creating breathtaking images and architectural marvels.

These artisans never approached their task with the thought of creating an object of beauty. For them, it was an act of faith and spiritual invocation, a way of manifesting the divine on Earth. Every delicate curve, every intricate crevice, every play of light and shadow was thoughtfully designed to evoke a sense of divinity.

7.2. Tools and Techniques: A Material Conduit

For these artisans, their tools were an extension of their being, a bridge between their physical existence and the spiritual realm. They consisted of simple implements — rammers, beaters, mallets, points, chisels, boasters, and claw chisels. While these tools have evolved over time technologically, their underlying essence — as bridges of faith — has remained unchanged.

The working process was one of unhurried dedication. Scaffolding was erected around the stone, and an intricate framework was marked using ropes, chalks, and rudimentary compasses. Each artisan worked in harmony with others. The first layer of rough sculpturewas chiseled out. Then, the stone was delicately smoothed and refined into the recognizable forms of gods and goddesses. In the final stages, details were added, transforming the stone into a mirror of divine beauty.

7.3. The Artisans: The Nameless Constructors of Divinity

These master craftsmen often hailed from the communities of Vishwakarmas, Stapathis, or Shilpis and were guided by profound iconographic texts such as Manasara Silpasastra, Shilparatna, and the Vastusutra Upanishad. Training was intensive and began at an early age, turning the craft into an integral part of their existence. The ability to shape divinity from stone was much more than a skill; it was a divine calling.

The apprenticeship lasted for years, and the knowledge was passed down from generation to generation, creating a unique bond between the master and the student. The identities of these artisans were never recorded. Their names do not feature on the walls they sculpted. They remain in anonymity. Yet, their work resonates through millennia.

7.4. The Impact of These Artful Creations

The marvels produced by these unknown craftsmen have traversed centuries, bearing the trauma of invasions, natural disasters, and the ravages of time. They stand today as a tangible link to the past, offering a window into a world where spirituality, art, and skilled craftsmanship were seamlessly intertwined. They continue to inspire awe, admiration, and provide serene sanctuaries.

One cannot help but feel a deep sense of awe and admiration when standing before such excellently crafted sculptures, silent yet powerful testimonies of the artisans' unparalleled skill and spiritual devotion. In the sheer majesty of stone comes a sense of the profound that goes beyond the mundanity of life, stirring the spirit within.

Dive deeper into the annals of history and immerse yourself in the astonishing tales of these temples carved out of devotion, faith, and love for the divine by purchasing this Special Report. Through these pages, embark on a journey of discovery, where spirituality, art, and human determination intertwined, resulting in masterpieces that continue to inspire and mesmerize us. Let these stories of the artisans who shaped divinity in stone guide you in your understanding and appreciation of human heritage and cultural depth. Surely, you wouldn't want to miss this incredible journey through time and space, where stone, chisel, and faith intersected to create miracles of architecture.

Chapter 8. Mother Nature's Canvas: Effects of Natural Elements on Carved Temples

In the grand tapestry of human achievement, temples carved directly from the living stone stand as towering testaments to our species' enduring devotion and adaptability. These sacred testaments, however, do not stand alone in their silent vigil. They engage in a perpetual dance with the environment—a dialogue between the carved stone and the very elements that shaped them.

8.1. The Architectural Symphony with the Elements

Considering the sheer scale and sophistication of these structures, it is humbling to reflect on the fact that they were hand-carved from solid rock, embarking on an eternally ongoing dialog with nature's elements. Over time, the wind, water, changing temperatures, and even biological activity have shaped the temples' aesthetic, forever altering their surfaces, colors, and structural integrity.

Wind, for instance, is a master sculptor. Over centuries, the persistent winds carve out intricate details on these monuments, etching out lines, crevices, and even dramatic changes in the facial profiles of the deities. Likely unintended by the original artisans, these alterations born from the wind breathe a unique life into the carvings, turning static stone into evolving canvases of history.

8.2. Water: A Tale of Erosion and Preservation

On the other hand, water—an essential requisite for life, presents a dichotomy of destruction and preservation in relation to stone-carved temples. The slow but continuous process of weathering wreaks havoc on the intricate designs and elaborate carvings, wearing them down, eroding the details, and altering the structural integrity of these colossal masterpieces.

However, water plays a distinctly contrary role as well. Evidence indicates that certain temples were specifically designed with water in mind, utilizing it as a protective measure. Water channels and draining systems were often incorporated into temple architecture to preserve the stone, utilizing nature's own force to safeguard from erosion.

8.3. The Chase of Temperatures

Temperature fluctuations, particularly in extreme conditions, can cause the stone to weather at an inconsistent rate, leading to a unique form of texturing. Bitter cold winters can cause the stone to contract while scorching summers cause it to expand, giving birth to openings and cracks that mar the surface over time but offer a certain character and personality to the stone. The interplay of temperature and carved temples gives each monument a unique "fingerprint," a weathered snapshot of the years passed.

8.4. The Muted Story by Biological Activities

In addition to these abiotic agents, the slow churn of life itself has influenced these structures. Lichens grow in patches, painting the stone in hues of green and red. The roots of persistent plants work their way into tiny crevices, their growth inexorably forcing the rock apart. Bird droppings, rich in acidic content, discolor the stone over time and, on occasion, erode sections of it. This biological activity, often overlooked compared to the more aggressive weathering forces, adds its own blend of colors, textures, and character to the stone tapestry.

In one notable example, the Kailasa Temple at Ellora in India, the ruinous effects of weathering have been largely mitigated thanks to the presence of bats. Amidst the carved sanctums, these creatures roost, their guano acting as a protective layer for the sensitive stone artworks underneath.

8.5. The Timeless Dialogue

In this ongoing, timeless dialogue, the elements have acted as the devoted custodians of these incredible sanctuaries, altering their appearance, and adding layers of meaning to their existence. They narrate a story that continues to be penned—an embrace of the forces which worked against their very creation.

To witness the effect of natural elements on these timeless marvels is akin to observing the drama of life itself. It's a testament to the impermanency of existence and the enduring will to create amidst transience. It's here that mankind's chiseled devotion interweaves with Mother Nature's canvas, where the spectrum of resist and yield, destruct and protect, stubborn endurance and graceful surrender can be seen and felt.

Chapter 9. Preserving History: Conservation and Restoration Efforts

The story of carved temples across the world is one filled with astonishing detail, beauty, and ancient wisdom. This legacy of craft, religion, and deep-seated belief faced the inevitable degradation that comes with time, yet it has weathered the storm and stayed resilient. The survival of these architectural masterpieces is thanks in large to the painstaking endeavor of committed conservators and restorers whose lifes' work has been to uphold the memories etched in stone, ensuring the splendors of old continue to inspire generations.

9.1. The Task of Preservation

Thinking about the task of preserving our architectural heritage brings us face to face with the enormity of the challenge at hand. From minute intricacies of ornate embellishments, to the imposing grandeur of stone structures, each aspect needs individual attention and specialist knowledge. Methodologies and courses of action in conservation are conditioned by considerations for preservation, aesthetics, historical authenticity, and respect for the original artist's or craftsperson's intention.

Conservation and restoration require a deep understanding of the original construction methods, materials used, the surrounding environment which has a bearing on the long-term effects on stone, and perhaps most importantly, the cultural and spiritual significance of the edifice. The scope of conservation involves safeguarding the physical fabric of the site, architectural detailing, artwork, and auxiliary elements that contribute to its overall perception.

Consider, for instance, the ancient rock temples in India, where the intricate carvings speak volumes of dedicated craftsmanship. Each figure, each line, and each curve requires meticulous attention to detail during restoration. The weathering has rendered some details almost invisible. Thus, conservators must walk a fine line between renewing the visibility of these details and ensuring they do not interfere with the authenticity of the craft.

9.2. Techniques in Conservation and Restoration

There are several key techniques employed in the conservation and restoration of stone structures. Laser cleaning is a common methodology. This technology enables the conservator to remove soot, dust, and other forms of pollution engrained on the stone without causing any physical damage to the underlying structures.

Another method is the consolidation of weakened stone. Materials such as ethyl silicate are used to strengthen the stone and mitigate weathering while maintaining its original appearance.

In circumstances where the stone is so worn that it threatens the structural integrity of the building, a process known as indenting is carried out. New stone of a similar appearance and properties is shaped to fit the original structure, providing improved strength while maintaining aesthetics.

The choice of conservation technique often hinges on the type of stone and the degree of degradation. For instance, the conservation of limestone structures like Egypt's pyramids involves the challenge of dealing with a very porous stone, susceptible to erosion and dissolution. On the other hand, granite structures demand strategies to deal with its porphyritic structure, where weathering can lead to flaking or granular disintegration.

9.3. The Role of Modern Technology

Advancements in technology have significantly aided the processes of conservation and restoration. Beyond the clinical application of lasers for cleaning, technologies such as 3D imaging and photogrammetry allow for intricate documentation of sites. This documentation forms an invaluable resource to track changes over time, plan conservation campaigns, and even recreate parts of the structure in virtual or physical mediums.

Software enabled structural analysis helps in understanding the stability of these structures and preemptively addresses risks of collapse or deterioration. Satellite imagery and remote sensing can be used to monitor large sites or clusters of monuments, ensuring their integrity over time.

9.4. The Ethical Considerations

Within the practice of architectural conservation, ethical considerations are as important as technical ones. Every intervention in a monument must respect its historical context and authenticity. From a conservation standpoint, we are not merely treating stone, but we are dealing with centuries of human endeavor, belief, and cultural expression.

There is an implicit understanding that any alteration to the site must be as minimal as possible, reversible if necessary, and should not distort the historical narrative. Past interventions have sometimes led to controversies when restorers have overstepped their role and made additions or modifications based on their own interpretations. These are considered false historical statements and are discouraged in modern practice.

9.5. Climate Change and Conservation

Another pressing concern in the field of architectural conservation is the rising impact of climate change. Changing patterns in rainfall, increased instances of extreme weather, and rising pollution levels are rapidly affecting the survivability of stone structures.

In response, modern conservation efforts have shifted towards proactive 'preventive conservation'. This approach strives to create stable environments that reduce or mitigate the risks to heritage sites. It's a synergistic process incorporating routine maintenance, monitoring, and implementing preventive measures, thereby prolonging the structure's life and conserving our global heritage.

The story of our carved temples is also the story of how we, as a society, value and uphold our cultural heritage. As we strive to preserve these marvels from our past, we are constantly reminded of the deep undercurrent of devotion that exists within us. Architectural conservation and restoration, therefore, stand as testimonies not just to our past, but also to our boundless capacity for preservation, reverence, and respect towards our shared human heritage.

Chapter 10. In the Hearts of the Devotees: Modern Day Significance

Sights of ardent worshippers gathered in front of these elaborately carved temples, lips moving in silent prayer, eyes glazed over with divine intoxication, can be seen now just as they have been for centuries. The remarkable persistence of devotion tied to these timeless edifices is a testament to their enduring spiritual significance. Despite the relentless march of technology and modernization, the original essence of these architecturally triumphant gems of devotion remains untarnished.

10.1. The Timeless Beacon of Faith

As the rising sun casts its gentle rays on the sculpted figures dancing on the stone facades, the temples awaken for another day of worship. Each morning, the sonorous bell rings in the air, punctuating the stillness and calling devotees to their pious observance. The scent of incense fills the hallways, intermingling with the faint aroma of stone, age, and a thousand prayers. The elaborate rituals performed by the devoted temple priests are a captivating dance of faith, love, and reverence, echoing the timeless practices recorded in ancient texts.

These rituals and ceremonies are not mere performances; they are an active bridge, connecting the past to the present, the mortal to the divine. In every anointing of the deity, every chant sung, every offering made, the temple's resonance with the devotees' present is solidified.

10.2. Unaltered Customs, Unwavering Devotion

Despite the rapid transformations in the outer world, the traditions practiced within the serene confines of these temples remain steadfast. Devotees continue to adhere to customs passed down over centuries, resonating with the shared pulse of collective belief. Whether it's the ritualistic bathing of the deity at dawn, the elaborate processions during annual festivals, or the night-time rituals to put the deity to sleep, each rite is performed meticulously, echoing past eras. This devotion rooted in ancient wisdom and time-honored practices renders an aura of tranquility and spirituality that transcends the mere physicality of the stone structure.

10.3. Representations of Devotion: Temple Art and Aesthetics

The interiors of these ancient temples often depict tales from mythology. Intricately etched on the temple walls are forms of divine entities, mythical creatures, and legendary warriors. These are not just stunning visual narratives; they serve a deeper, symbolic purpose. They represent the ideals, morals, and wisdom of the faith. Marveled and studied intensely by the devotees, these beautiful inscriptions become a medium of instruction, imparting moral and spiritual lessons in a most splendid manner.

10.4. Spiritual Energy: A Divine Connection

Beyond the rituals, beyond the mythological stories etched on the stone walls, people find an energetic spiritual vibration that resonates with their faith. Many describe it as an immediate sense of peace, a transcendental experience, or a divine connection felt upon setting foot within these hallowed walls. This spiritual energy, suffused within every chiseled detail, is often cited by devotees as a constant source of strength and serenity, a sanctuary from worldly chaos. The collective aura of belief and the pervading sense of peace serve to establish a unique, timeless bond between the devotee and the divine manifestation carved in stone.

10.5. Sacred Festivals: A Testament to Enduring Faith

It is during religious festivals that the latent pulse of these ancient edifices truly comes alive. Swirling in the air is an undeniable energy, an excitement accentuated by the sudden vibrancy of colors, the constant sound of music, and the influx of devotees from all walks of life. There is a palpable sense of unity during these festivals as distinct barriers of status, wealth, and profession dissolve in the collective celebration of faith. These annual observances are a testament to the enduring faith and devotion of worshippers, an affirmation of the ageless role of these temples as cultural and spiritual epicenters.

With the dawn of each day, the faith and devotion held within these monumental temples stand resolute in the face of the ceaseless tide of time. Even as the modern world continues its march towards an increasingly digital reality, these temples firmly anchor human spirituality in tangible, exquisitely chiseled stone. They serve as invaluable repositories of cultural and religious practices, narrating ancient tales of wisdom and piety, echoing the robust faith of devotees across generations and modern-day contexts.

In the end, it's not just the grandeur of these temples' architecture that makes them an invaluable part of our shared human heritage. The continued significance lies equally, if not more, in their ability to inspire, to resonate with countless hearts, to foster a profound sense of spiritual connection, and to reaffirm faith. The imprint of the ancient chisel on stone continues to be mirrored in the hearts of the devotees, etching tales of unwavering devotion and perennial faith. It is in this ongoing legacy of devotion that these ancient architectural marvels find their true modern-day significance.

Chapter 11. The Silent Monologue of Stone: Lessons from Carved Temples

Condensing the grandeur of ancient carved temples into words, their stories, their legacy, their teachings, is a task of its own. Customarily mute, these structures narrate tales of the past, teaching us humility and the power of human dedication, bound by faith and a will to create art in its truest forms. Today, we step into these timeless edifices, listening attentively to their silent monologue.

11.1. Entering the Stone Matrix

An entry into these stone havens is akin to plunging into an entirely different universe. The air feels heavy but comforting, bearing staleness of the centuries past, mingled with a sense of divine presence. The first impression is often of a labyrinth sculpted in stone; every wall, column, and ceiling filled with intricate carvings, each telling a separate tale, yet they're a part of one grand narrative, celebrating human devotion. But more than a panorama of religious fervor, these carvings demonstrate the merge of human imagination with tangible matter.

11.2. Stories Whispered By the Stone Walls

As one steps deeper into the stone matrix, the sheer detail and labor poured into these works of art become palpity palpable. The walls, etched with images of gods, goddesses, and an assortment of celestial beings, speak volumes about cultural ideologies of the times. The hierarchies of the deities depicted, the varying expressions, the proportions, and odd symbology – they all whisper a story meant for those who listen.

The artistry is not purely religious. The everyday life scenes carved into these walls provide invaluable glimpses into the past. The varied narratives encompassing war, trade, courtly love, justice, music, and dance reflect the societal organization, moral values, music, lifestyle, and the incredible echoes from the golden era of human civilization.

11.3. The Anatomy of a Carved Temple

The design of these temples provides a divine experience of navigating through an architectural masterpiece. The main sanctum sanctorum, the 'Garbhagriha', is the nucleus of the temple, housing the presiding deity. Flanked by a series of other smaller sanctum, passage-like structures and open platforms called the 'Mandapams', it seems to draw the visitor's gravity towards the center. The gradual progression through these compartments, each adorned with elaborate carvings, amplifies the divine experience. The temple top, the 'shikhara', punctuates the sky, an attempt to bridge the gap between heaven and earth.

11.4. Secrets of the Stonemasons

Every carved temple acknowledges the human endeavor of translating spiritual energy into stone. Those who set chisel to stone were not mere artisans – they were storytellers, they were poets, they were philosophers. Their understanding of stone transcended material boundaries, enabling them to breathe life into inanimate rocks. These masons brought not just architectural proficiency, but an understanding of material properties, mathematics, astronomy, and sacred geometry to their art. The allegory of the cosmos and its order running through their conceptualization and execution is nothing short of remarkable.

They followed a noble tradition called the 'Sthapatya Veda' or the Vedic system of architecture. The cryptic concept of carving temples out of a single rock, also known as 'monolithic architecture', required nothing short of divine guidance. Yet these stonemasons achieved it, and their legacy persists, leaving behind lessons of dedication, craftsmanship, and profound faith.

11.5. The Resounding Echoes

Despite the stillness, these temples seem to resonate with a unique energy. It's a power that emanates from their silent monologues, echoing celestial chants, imparting profound spiritual vibrations. Partly due to their sacred nature and the palpable sense of reverence they command, partly due to their construction, these edifices serve more than religious pilgrimage sites – they are time capsules, resonating with an ageless melody that attunes us all to our shared human heritage.

These temples stand as a testament to humanity's quest to express its spirituality and its desire to foster a sense of shared cultural identity. They silently echo their creators' pursuit of artistic excellence and their keen observance of divine principles. Their silent monologue remains a constant, narrating the saga of past glory, present wisdom, and future possibilities.

Whether one embraces them as marvels of human craftsmanship, mementos of cultural heritage, or beacons of spiritual inspiration, these carved temples continue to whisper tales to anyone willing to listen. They stand tall, etching their silhouettes against the horizon, a timeless manifestation of mankind's chiseled devotion: a symphony etched in stone.

11.6. Conclusion

To step into these carved temples is to step into a space carved by an uncompromising reverence for artistic expression and spirituality. A step into these sacred spaces is, in many ways, a step into our shared past, a step into the heart of our collective heritage. Let us, therefore, continue to learn, to be inspired by their silent monologue, and continue to revere these stone chronicles of human devotion.

www.ingramcontent.com/pod-product-compliance
Lightning Source LLC
Chambersburg PA
CBHW060856260726
48661CB00008B/3301